HOW TO START SONG WRITING BUSINESS

The 6- Figure Song Writer's Guide to Fame

Jeanelle K. Douglas

Copyright © 2024 by Jeanelle K. Douglas. All rights reserved.

DEDICATION

To the reader who holds this book. You hold the key to unlocking this journey.

Thank you for joining me.

Table of Contents

Introduction 7
- Exploring the Components of a Song 9
- Understanding Song Structure and Form 12
- Analyzing Successful Songs: Case Studies 16
- Finding Your Unique Voice as a Songwriter 18
- Developing Your Songwriting Skills 21
- The Importance of Practice and Persistence 23

Techniques for Overcoming Writer's Block 26
- Improving Lyric Writing: From Poetry to Song 28
- Enhancing Melody Creation and Harmony 29
- Experimenting with Song Arrangement and Instrumentation ... 32

Navigating the Music Industry Landscape 34
- Overview of the Music Industry: Roles and Players 37
- Understanding Copyrights and Royalties 40
- Exploring Music Publishing and Licensing 42
- Building Relationships: Networking in the Industry 44
- Resources for Songwriters: Organizations and Tools 46

Crafting Your Professional Identity 49
- Defining Your Artistic Brand 52

- Creating a Compelling Artist Persona 55
- Designing Your Online Presence: Website and Social Media .. 57
- Promotional Strategies for Independent Songwriters 59
- Collaborating with Other Artists and Producers 63

Recording and Producing Your Music 65
- Mixing and Mastering Your Tracks 67
- Setting Up a Home Studio on a Budget 69
- Basics of Audio Recording and Production 73
- Working with Session Musicians and Producers 76
- Distributing Your Music: Digital Platforms and Physical Releases 79
- Music Publishing Negotiation 82

Building a Fanbase and Generating Income 85
- Engaging with Your Audience: Live Performances and Online Interaction 88
- Strategies for Growing Your Fanbase: Social Media, Email Lists, and Merchandise 91
- Monetizing Your Music: Streaming Revenue, Merchandising, and Live Gigs 94
- Exploring Opportunities in Sync Licensing and Film/TV Placements 96

Maximizing Revenue Streams: Diversification and Financial Management 99

Sustaining Long-Term Success in Songwriting 103

The Importance of Continual Learning and Growth 106

Overcoming Challenges in the Music Industry 109

Nurturing Your Creativity and Passion 112

Balancing Artistic Integrity with Commercial Viability 115

Leaving a Lasting Impact: Legacy and Influence in Songwriting
.... 118

Introduction

In the ever-changing environment of the music industry, songwriting is a timeless profession, a brilliant blending of poetry and melody with the ability to captivate hearts, inspire minds, and transcend cultural barriers. Every chart-topping single, iconic ballad, and soul-stirring lyric is the product of a songwriter's creative talent.

The transformational power of songwriting can be witnessed firsthand when you are carried away by a song's charm, touched by its lyrics, or caught up in its melody. Perhaps you've even considered making a profession out of creating your own musical masterpieces and sharing your experiences with the world via the universal language of music.

This book is a comprehensive guide specifically created for ambitious songwriters like yourself who aspire to elevate their passion for music. This book will guide you to success in the world of songwriting, whether you're a new composer just getting started or a seasoned artist trying to transform your passion for music into a rewarding profession.

These pages provide a wealth of knowledge, ideas, and practical guidance gleaned from the experience of seasoned songwriters, industry insiders, and music professionals. From comprehending the fundamental building blocks of songwriting to navigating the convoluted routes of the music industry, from perfecting your skill to growing your brand and fans, this book covers every facet of starting and maintaining a successful songwriting career. But this book is more than simply a guide for budding songwriters; it is a voyage through imagination, passion, and the quest for musical brilliance.

It's a celebration of the art and skill of songwriting, as well as a monument to music's eternal ability to touch hearts, transform lives, and influence our surroundings. So, whether you want to write chart-topping singles, play on stages all over the world, or just share your music with anybody who will listen, let this book lead you through this thrilling and gratifying journey into the heart of songwriting. Let's make your musical ambitions a reality.

Let's start creating the soundtrack to your life!!

Exploring the Components of a Song

Exploring the Parts of a Song Before going into the complex realm of songwriting, it's critical to grasp the fundamental elements that comprise a song. A composer combines numerous components to develop a fascinating musical composition, much as a painter uses colors to create a masterpiece or an architect uses different materials to construct a structure. These components interact together to elicit emotions, transmit messages, and make an indelible impact on listeners.

First and foremost, each song starts with a fundamental idea or concept, a basic topic that drives the words and music. This might be a personal experience, a universal feeling, or a thought-provoking narrative that connects with both the artist and their audience. The topic gives the song depth and purpose, directing the creative process and molding the ultimate message.

The lyrics come next, and they serve as a linguistic embodiment of the song's concept. Lyrics can vary from basic and plain to lyrical and metaphorical, depending on the songwriter's style and goal. They use vivid visuals, complex emotions, and fascinating storytelling to captivate the listener's imagination. Writing effective songs takes careful consideration of word choice, rhythm, and rhyme scheme, as well as an awareness of story structure and poetic elements.

The melody is a succession of musical notes that accompany the lyrics and give voice to the songwriter's words. The melody is the essence of the song, conveying the emotional weight and creating the tone for listeners. It may be catchy and lively, mournful and haunting, or anywhere in between, depending on the songwriter's creative vision. Creating a memorable tune requires experimentation, intuition, a strong ear for music, and knowledge of scales, intervals, and chord progressions.

In addition to lyrics and melody, songs frequently include musical accompaniment, which adds depth and complexity to the music. This can contain a variety of instruments, such as guitars and pianos, as well as drums and violins, each of which adds its own sound and character to the overall composition. The arrangement of various instruments, known as the song's instrumentation, is critical in establishing the auditory environment and increasing the emotional effect.

The song's structure governs the grouping and presentation of its many components to listeners. Common song forms include verse-chorus, verse-bridge-chorus, and AABA, each of which provides a unique framework for storytelling and melodic growth. The framework lends consistency and development to the song, leading listeners through its narrative arc and emphasizing its major ideas.

Beyond the fundamental aspects of lyrics, melody, instrumentation, and structure, aspiring songwriters must dig into the details of each component and grasp how they work together to produce a coherent and captivating musical composition.

Lyrics, for example, are more than simply a collection of words; they are a type of narrative that allows songwriters to communicate their thoughts, feelings, and experiences in a meaningful and accessible manner. Aspiring songwriters might benefit from mastering the art of lyric writing, which involves using poetic methods such as metaphor, simile, imagery, and symbolism to create songs that connect with listeners on a deeper level.

Similarly, melody is the emotional foundation of a song, communicating mood and atmosphere via the rise and fall of musical notes. Aspiring songwriters can use several melodic methods, including contour, intervallic structure, and rhythmic variation, to produce melodies that are memorable and expressive. Instrumentation shapes a song's overall tone and feel, providing layers of depth and complexity to the musical arrangement. Aspiring composers can experiment with varied instrumental textures, dynamics, and arrangements to increase the emotional impact of their tunes and develop a distinct musical identity.

Structure is also an important part of songwriting that may significantly impact the listener's experience. Aspiring composers might experiment with various song forms, such as verse-chorus, AABA, or through-composed, to produce songs that flow organically and keep listeners engaged from beginning to end. Budding songwriters might benefit from examining professional songwriters' work and evaluating their compositions to learn how they effectively use these elements to produce memorable and meaningful songs. By learning a variety of musical genres and styles, prospective songwriters may broaden their creative horizons and build their own distinct voice as authors.

Understanding Song Structure and Form

Comprehending a building's design before it is built is analogous to understanding music structure and shape. It acts as the foundation for the whole piece, directing the flow of musical ideas and structuring the listener's experience from start to finish. At its foundation, song structure is the arrangement of a song's numerous sections, such as verses, choruses, bridges, and instrumental breaks, into a coherent and compelling whole. While there are numerous varieties and permutations of song patterns, several popular forms have arisen over time, each with their own distinct qualities and customs.

The verse-chorus form is one of the most common song forms, consisting of alternating verses and choruses that serve as the song's main narrative and emotional focal points, respectively. Passages usually comprise poetic passages that develop the song's plot or communicate certain emotions, whereas choruses have repeating, memorable melodies and lyrics that act as the song's hook or main message.

The AABA form is another common song structure that follows a more linear sequence of musical ideas, with a verse followed by a contrasting bridge part before returning to the same verse content. Composers widely find this form in jazz standards and classic pop songs, providing them with a flexible foundation for creating intricate melodies and harmonies.

In addition to these standard forms, songwriters frequently experiment with more unusual structures, such as through-composed or episodic forms, which reject typical verse-chorus norms in favor of a more fluid and dynamic approach to songwriting. These forms provide greater freedom and flexibility in creating songs that challenge traditional assumptions and push the boundaries of musical expression. Regardless of the style or structure used, great songwriting necessitates a thorough grasp of how these components interact to generate a unified and captivating musical story.

Aspiring songwriters might benefit from studying and analyzing professional songwriters' compositions to learn how they use song structure and form to produce memorable and meaningful songs. Knowing song structure and form is required for successful communication with other musicians, producers, and collaborators during the songwriting and recording processes. Songwriters can ensure the accomplishment of their creative vision and the alignment of all collaborators towards the same objective by expressing their ideas in terms of song structure and form.

A thorough knowledge of song structure and form is essential for songwriting success, whether you're producing catchy pop hits, introspective ballads, or experimental masterpieces.

Understanding song structure and form is more than just following a set of rules; it's about using music to convey stories. Each element of a song, whether a verse, chorus, bridge, or instrumental break, plays a specific role in moving the story along and eliciting emotional reactions from listeners. Verses, for example, frequently serve as the foundation for the song's plot, introducing people, situations, and themes through detailed lyrics and melodies. They give background and create anticipation for the chorus, which is the song's emotional climax, conveying the fundamental message or hook in a memorable and compelling manner. Throughout the song, the chorus frequently repeats, emphasizing its importance and ensuring that it remains in the listener's memory long after the song has concluded.

Bridges, on the other hand, provide a break from the conventional verse-chorus structure by introducing new musical ideas, topics, or viewpoints that add depth and complexity to the song. They give a brief respite from the repetition of verses and choruses, giving listeners a new viewpoint and keeping them interested from beginning to end. Instrumental breaks, such as solos or interludes, allow instrumentalists to demonstrate their abilities and add dynamic diversity to the song.

They can act as tension relief after a particularly dramatic chorus or as a transition between sections, allowing the music to flow smoothly from one to the next. By comprehending how each portion of a song contributes to its overall structure and narrative arc, prospective songwriters may successfully control these aspects to produce songs that are both musically rewarding and emotionally impactful.

They can experiment with alternative verses, choruses, bridges, and instrumental breaks to achieve the ideal mix of repetition and diversity, tension and relaxation, which will keep listeners engaged from beginning to end. Mastering song structure and form helps prospective songwriters successfully express their creative ideas to other musicians, producers, and collaborators.

Analyzing Successful Songs: Case Studies

Analyzing successful songs is one of the most effective learning tools for anyone interested in establishing a songwriting career. By examining and studying the compositions of well-known composers, aspiring songwriters can obtain significant insights into the approaches, structures, and factors that contribute to a song's popularity. Case studies provide an exceptional chance to dig deeply into the inner workings of a song, studying its lyrics, melody, instrumentation, structure, and overall effect on listeners.

Choosing a broader selection of popular songs from various genres, styles, and eras, budding composers may extend their musical horizons and draw inspiration from a number of sources. For example, a case study of a timeless pop hit like The Beatles' "Yesterday" might demonstrate the importance of simplicity in composition. Through its heartbreaking lyrics, evocative melody, and stripped-down arrangement, "Yesterday" exemplifies how a song may connect with listeners on a global level by tapping into comparable feelings and experiences.

On the other side, a case study of a modern success, such as Ed Sheeran's "Shape of You," might demonstrate the value of creativity and experimentation in songwriting. With its addictive beat, catchy hooks, and fusion of pop, R&B, and dancehall elements, "Shape of You" demonstrates how crossing genre and style barriers can result in a fresh and interesting musical composition. In addition, a case study of a great rock hymn, such as "Stairway to Heaven" by Led Zeppelin, may demonstrate the skill of storytelling and narrative progression in composition. "Stairway to Heaven" transports listeners on a voyage of reflection and investigation, demonstrating music's ability to transcend borders and elicit powerful emotions. By studying these and other popular songs, prospective composers might discover repeating patterns, approaches, and tactics that contribute to their success.

They can examine the relationship between words and melody, the use of instruments and arrangements to create mood and atmosphere, and how structure and form contribute to the song's overall influence on listeners. Furthermore, case studies might encourage prospective songwriters to experiment with their own compositions, bringing components and strategies learned from successful songs into their own creative processes. By studying the works of established songwriters and applying their insights to their own songs, prospective songwriters may refine their craft, broaden their artistic horizons, and, ultimately, boost their chances of success in the competitive world of songwriting.

Finding Your Unique Voice as a Songwriter

Finding Your Unique Voice as a Songwriter In the broad and diverse realm of music, each composer has a distinct voice, an artistic fingerprint that distinguishes them from their contemporaries. This distinct voice reflects their own personality, experiences, and worldview. Discovering and cultivating this voice is critical for prospective songwriters seeking to launch a career in music.

Finding your distinctive voice as a composer is really about being honest and true to yourself. It's about delving into your deepest ideas, feelings, and experiences and expressing them through your music in a true and honest manner. It is about having the guts to be vulnerable, to share your truth with the world, and to connect with your audience on a deep and personal level.

Self-discovery is one of the first stages in developing your own voice as a composer. This entails investigating your own interests, hobbies, and life experiences and reflecting on how these form your viewpoint and impact your artistic expression. What themes and subjects resonate with you on a personal level? Which emotions do you find yourself drawn to when creating music? Delving into these questions can help you discover the core of your own songwriting voice.

Experimentation is also a vital part of discovering your distinctive voice as a songwriter.

This entails getting out of your comfort zone, attempting new things, and stretching the limits of your imagination. Do not be hesitant to experiment with diverse musical styles, genres, and methods or to incorporate aspects from other creative forms into your music. Experimenting with different songwriting styles allows you to uncover new aspects of your artistic personality and establish your own distinct style. Furthermore, discovering your distinct voice as a songwriter necessitates continuous self-reflection and development.

This means regularly reviewing your work, soliciting input from others, and making changes as necessary to remain loyal to your artistic vision. It's about perfecting your art, sharpening your talents, and aiming for perfection in all you do as a composer. In addition to self-discovery, experimenting, and self-reflection, creating your distinctive voice as a composer entails accepting your flaws and the process of growth and evolution.

It's about understanding that your voice as a songwriter is not static but rather evolves and changes with time. Don't be afraid to embrace the road of self-discovery and self-expression, as well as the beauty of imperfection, as you seek to create your own unique voice as a composer.

Discovering your distinctive voice as a songwriter is a very personal and transforming experience. It's about being yourself, pursuing your hobbies and ambitions, trying new songwriting styles, and always honing your art. By being loyal to yourself and embracing the process of self-discovery and self-expression, you may uncover your distinct voice as a songwriter and begin a rewarding career in music.

Developing Your Songwriting Skills

Developing your songwriting skills Starting a songwriting career needs more than simply skill; it necessitates devotion, perseverance, and a commitment to continual growth and progress. Developing your songwriting talents is an important stage in this journey because it lays the groundwork for generating captivating and memorable music that appeals to people. Immersion in music is one of the first stages in developing your songwriting talents.

Listen to a range of genres, styles, and musicians, paying special attention to the methods, structures, and aspects that distinguish each song. Examine the lyrics, melody, instrumentation, and arrangement of your favorite songs, and evaluate how these aspects combine to form a cohesive and interesting musical composition. In addition, research the work of prominent songwriters and songwriting strategies. Read books, articles, and interviews on songwriting, attend workshops and seminars, and look for mentors and partners who may provide advice and support.

Learning from others' experiences and perspectives might provide you with vital knowledge and inspiration for your own songwriting practice. Practice is another important component of honing your songwriting abilities. Set aside time each day or week to develop and improve your songs, experiment with different lyrical and melodic concepts, and learn new musical methods and genres. Don't be afraid to create numerous drafts of a song or to go back and rework your work until you're happy with the outcome. The more you practice, the more you'll progress and grow closer to discovering your own voice as a songwriter. Collaboration is also essential for improving your songwriting talents. Look for ways to work with other musicians, lyricists, and producers, and be open to feedback and constructive criticism.

Working with others not only broadens your creative horizons but also helps you learn from other viewpoints and experiences, therefore improving your own songwriting talents. Furthermore, don't underestimate the value of feedback and constructive criticism for your songwriting progress. Share your work with friends, family, fellow songwriters, and music industry experts to get their opinions and thoughts. Be open to criticism and eager to learn from both positive and negative feedback, and use it to inform and improve your next songwriting project.

Remember that honing your songwriting talents is a lifetime process. As a composer, you should always be interested, hungry, and eager to learn and improve. Whether you're just starting out or have been creating music for years, there's always potential for growth and new discoveries. Accept the process of growth and evolution and allow it to guide you on your journey to becoming a successful composer. Finally, honing your songwriting talents is an important step in launching a songwriting profession. Immersing yourself in music, studying the work of established songwriters, practicing regularly, collaborating with others, seeking feedback and constructive criticism, and accepting the process of growth and evolution will allow you to hone your craft, refine your skills, and embark on a fulfilling and successful music career.

The Importance of Practice and Persistence

The Value of Practice and Persistence Starting a songwriting career is an exciting, creative adventure with limitless potential. However, like any art or job, success in songwriting necessitates a great deal of practice and perseverance.

These two factors are the driving forces behind any prospective songwriter's growth and development:

Developing their artistic talents: Perfecting their craft, and eventually moving them toward their objectives. Songwriting, like any other creative pursuit, relies heavily on practice to improve skills. A composer, like a musician, must practice their art in order to hone their talents and unlock their creative potential. This entails devoting regular time and effort to creating and producing music, experimenting with various approaches and genres, and pushing the limits of one's creativity.

Practicing helps prospective songwriters build their own voice and artistic personality. Creating and developing their songs on a regular basis, students may explore their musical tastes, topics, and emotions while also beginning to build their own individual style. Through practice, students can experiment with new melodies, chord progressions, and lyrical approaches, eventually refining their works until they really reflect their creative vision.

Persistence: Is also essential in the process of developing a songwriting career. The route to success in music is rarely straight, and ambitious composers will undoubtedly face roadblocks, failures, and problems along the way. Ambitious songwriters continue in the face of adversity, whether they are coping with self-doubt and creative blockages, being rejected by record companies, or fighting to find an audience for their music, thanks to their persistence.

Persistence is what motivates them to keep creating, polishing, and moving forward, even when the odds appear stacked against them. It enables them to learn from their shortcomings, develop from their mistakes, and emerge as stronger and more resilient artists. It is the persistent resolve to pursue their passion and never give up on their aspirations that distinguishes individuals who aspire to begin a songwriting career from those who succeed.

Furthermore, perseverance leads to growth and advancement as a composer. By composing, revising, and perfecting their craft on a regular basis, aspiring songwriters may continue to improve their talents, broaden their artistic horizons, and achieve new heights of creativity and expression. Persistence is required to overcome creative obstacles, break past hurdles, and realize their full potential as songwriters. With practice and perseverance as their guiding principles, students may pursue a meaningful and successful career in music, sharing their tales and feelings with the world via the global language of song.

The music industry is fiercely competitive, and success frequently necessitates a mix of skill, hard work, and determination. By regularly practicing their art and following their goals, aspiring songwriters can gradually gather momentum, gain traction, and make progress toward their dreams. Consistency is essential for building a presence in the music industry, whether through regular song releases, live performances, or networking events. Ambitious songwriters who are dedicated to their art and maintain a regular presence can draw attention, acquire a fan base, and create opportunities for themselves in the music industry.

Techniques for Overcoming Writer's Block

Tips for Overcoming Writer's Block Writer's block is a typical problem that every composer encounters at some point in their lives. Songwriters often experience the frustrating sensation of being stuck, unable to generate fresh ideas or make progress on a song. However, ambitious songwriters may employ a variety of strategies to overcome writer's block and rediscover their inspiration. To overcome writer's block, take a breather and move away from the songwriting process for a bit.

Sometimes simply allowing yourself to take a break and focus on other things will help clear your thoughts and relieve the strain you may be placing on yourself to come up with ideas. Engage in activities that inspire you, such as taking a stroll in nature, listening to music, or reading. New ideas frequently strike you at the most unexpected times. Another option is to alter your surroundings. If you usually create music in the same spot, consider relocating to a different area to spark your creativity.

This may be as easy as relocating your home office to a local park or just changing the furniture in your working location. Changing your surroundings might help spice up your routine and spark fresh thoughts. Collaboration is another effective method of overcoming writer's block. Reach out to other composers, musicians, or producers to work on a song together. Working with people might bring new insights and ideas that you would not have considered on your own.

The act of collaborating might rekindle your enthusiasm for composing and motivate you to overcome writer's block. Experimenting with various songwriting styles might also help you overcome writer's block. If you usually compose the lyrics first, consider starting with the music instead, or vice versa. You may also try out alternative song structures, chord progressions, and rhythms to generate fresh ideas. Don't be scared to attempt new things and push yourself beyond your comfort zone.

Scheduling frequent writing sessions might help avoid writer's block in the first place. Establishing a steady writing habit and making songwriting a regular part of your calendar might help you keep your creativity flowing and avoid creative blockages. Treat songwriting as any other talent that needs practice and devotion, and commit to showing up and putting in the effort even when inspiration is scarce.

Writer's block is a typical difficulty for all songwriters, it does not have to stifle your creativity. Taking breaks, changing your environment, collaborating with others, experimenting with songwriting techniques, and establishing a consistent writing routine can help you overcome writer's block and keep your creativity flowing as you embark on your journey to start a songwriting career.

Improving Lyric Writing: From Poetry to Song

Enhancing lyric writing requires striking a balance between simplicity and intricacy. While it is crucial to successfully express meaning and emotion, using too sophisticated vocabulary or confusing metaphors might detract from the song's overall impact. Strive for clarity and accessibility in your lyrics, employing language that connects with listeners and conveys your message in a clear and sympathetic manner.

Paying attention to the musicality of your lyrics may significantly increase their efficacy. Consider how your lyrics' rhythm and cadence fit with the song's melody and phrase. Experiment with varying syllable counts, stresses, and vowel sounds to create lyrical patterns that flow naturally with the music, giving your song depth and character. Furthermore, do not overlook the importance of emotion in lyric composition. The finest songs generate an emotional response from listeners, whether it's happiness, grief, rage, or nostalgia. Tap into your personal emotions and experiences to make your lyrics more honest and sincere, helping listeners to connect with your music on a deeper level.

Don't be scared to experiment and push the limits of standard lyric composition. Experiment with unorthodox structures, surprising imagery, and creative language to produce songs that stand out and leave an impact. Accept your originality and trust your instincts as a composer, letting your own voice and viewpoint come through in your songs.

Enhancing Melody Creation and Harmony

Enhancing Melody Creation and Harmony Melody composition and harmony are key components of songwriting since they help to captivate listeners and express the emotions and thoughts inherent in a song. Aspiring songwriters who want to start a successful career should work on improving their talents in these areas in order to create unique and effective songs. Melody creation is the process of creating a series of musical notes that create the primary topic or tune of a song.

A powerful melody is not only catchy and memorable, but it also conveys the appropriate atmosphere and complements the song's verbal substance. To improve melody production, prospective songwriters might experiment with different scales and intervals, play with rhythm and phrasing, and take inspiration from a variety of musical genres and styles.

Researching and evaluating well-known song melodies can give useful insights into effective melody creation. Harmony, on the other hand, is the mixing of many musical notes performed or sung together to produce a pleasant sound. Harmonies give depth and richness to music, increasing its emotional effect while also generating a feeling of balance and cohesiveness. Aspiring composers can improve their grasp of harmony by studying chord progressions, voicings, and harmonic strategies like modulation and counterpoint.

Experimenting with various chord combinations and voicings may help aspiring songwriters expand their harmonic vocabulary and craft more dynamic and appealing tunes. Prospective songwriters can improve melody generation and harmony by focusing on the interaction between the melody and the underlying chords. A powerful melody should complement the chords and vice versa, resulting in a sense of wholeness and coherence throughout the song.

Understanding the basics of chord-scale connections and chord inversions may assist prospective composers in creating melodies that blend effortlessly with the underlying harmony, increasing the composition's overall musicality. Collaboration may also be an effective strategy for improving melody production and harmony. Working with other musicians, composers, or producers can bring new views and ideas for improving a song's melody and harmony.

Working with others may lead to unexpected musical discoveries and motivate prospective songwriters to push the limits of their creativity. Furthermore, playing with diverse instruments and arrangements helps improve melody development and harmony by adding texture and depth to a track. Aspiring songwriters can experiment with diverse instrumental combinations, layering methods, and production approaches to create distinct and engaging sonic environments that heighten the emotional impact of their works.

Ambitious songwriters who want to start a great music career must improve their melody composition and harmony skills. By experimenting with different approaches, examining the work of famous songwriters, working with others, and trying with diverse instruments and arrangements, aspiring songwriters may improve their talents and produce unique and compelling songs that resonate with audiences.

Experimenting with Song Arrangement and Instrumentation

Song arrangement and instrumentation are critical components in determining the overall sound and effect of a musical work. Aspiring composers who want to have a successful career must be prepared to experiment with diverse arrangements and instruments in order to develop distinctive and interesting songs that capture audiences. Song arrangement is the process of defining a song's structure and organization, including the placement of verses, choruses, bridges, and other sections.

Experimenting with song arrangement allows prospective composers to try out numerous methods to portray their musical ideas and storylines, resulting in shifts in dynamics, tension, and release throughout the song. Aspiring songwriters might experiment with song patterns such as verse-chorus-verse or AABA, as well as variations in speed, key changes, and instrumentation. They can also try different placements for instrumental breaks, solos, and outros to bring interest and variation to the song.

Instrumentation refers to the selection and use of musical instruments in a song, such as vocals, guitars, keyboards, drums, and so on. Experimenting with instrumentation enables aspiring songwriters to create distinct aural textures and emotions, bringing their musical concepts to life in novel and intriguing ways. Aspiring composers might experiment with instrumentation by comparing acoustic and electric guitars, piano and synthesizers, and live drumming with computer beats.

They can also experiment with the arrangement of instruments inside the song, such as layering various guitar recordings or including unusual instruments to create color and depth. Furthermore, prospective songwriters might experiment with instrumentation by combining components from many musical genres and styles into their works. For example, combining parts of rock, pop, folk, and electronic music may produce a unique and new sound that appeals to a wide range of listeners. Collaboration may also be an effective method for experimenting with song structure and instrumentation. Working with other musicians, producers, or arrangers can bring new views and ideas for improving a song's arrangement and instrumentation. Furthermore, working with others may lead to unexpected musical discoveries and motivate prospective songwriters to push the limits of their creativity.

Prospective songwriters can experiment with instruments and arrangements by using various production techniques and effects. Experimenting with reverb, delay, compression, and other audio effects may help the arrangement gain depth and dimension, improving the overall sound and impact of the song.

Navigating the Music Industry Landscape

Navigating the music industry landscape starting a songwriting career entails not just improving your talent but also navigating the complicated environment of the music industry. Understanding the many components of the industry, developing contacts, and effectively advertising your music are all necessary steps toward being a successful composer.

First and foremost, educate yourself on the many segments of the music industry. This involves knowing the responsibilities of record labels, publishers, distributors, agents, managers, and performance rights organizations (PROs) such as ASCAP, BMI, and SESAC. Each organization has a distinct purpose in the music ecosystem, and understanding how they work will help you make smart career decisions.

Building relationships is another important component of managing the music industry. Networking with fellow composers, musicians, producers, industry experts, and music fans may lead to new possibilities, collaborations, and mentoring. Attending industry events, conferences, workshops, and showcases allows you to network with people in the business and demonstrate your skills.

Understanding the financial side of the music industry is critical to my success as a writer. This involves an understanding of music publication, copyright legislation, royalties, licensing, and income sources. Familiarize yourself with the fundamentals of music publishing, such as publishers' roles in promoting and licensing your music, as well as the need to register your songs with PROs to ensure you earn royalties from public performances.

Promoting your music properly is also essential for navigating the music industry. This includes establishing a strong online presence via social media, streaming platforms, and your own website. Use services like SoundCloud, Spotify, YouTube, and Bandcamp to promote your music and communicate with listeners. Consider sending your music to blogs, playlists, and music discovery sites to boost awareness and reach new audiences. Collaboration is another effective method for managing the music industry.

Collaboration with other artists, producers, and industry experts may provide invaluable assistance, resources, and possibilities for progress. Collaboration on songwriting projects, co-writing with other songwriters, or working with producers can help improve the production quality of your music. Building a solid network of colleagues will help you broaden your horizons and achieve your creative ambitions.

Furthermore, remaining current with industry trends, advances, and opportunities is critical for navigating the ever-changing music industry landscape. Keep up with industry journals, blogs, podcasts, and emails to learn about new technology, developing trends, and possibilities for songwriters.

Additionally, look for educational materials, workshops, and seminars to expand your knowledge and abilities in songwriting and the music industry. Navigating the music industry landscape necessitates a combination of creativity, business acumen, and networking abilities. To navigate the music industry environment and establish yourself as a successful composer, you can benefit from understanding the many components of the industry, creating contacts, effectively advertising your music, working with others, and being educated about industry trends.

Overview of the Music Industry: Roles and Players

Starting a songwriting career requires knowing the music industry's complex ecology, which includes a variety of jobs and participants. Each company has a distinct function in music development, marketing, distribution, and monetization, all of which contribute to the industry's diverse and dynamic landscape.

The artist is a crucial actor in the music industry since he or she makes and performs music. Artists, whether alone or in bands, are in charge of composing songs, producing music, and presenting live shows. Aspiring songwriters frequently begin their careers as performers, utilizing their own performances to promote their unique songs and earn notoriety. Record labels are another critical component of the music industry, acting as the primary way of distributing and promoting music to the general public. Record companies negotiate contracts with artists, fund recording and production of their music, and oversee distribution, marketing, and promotion.

They play an important role in molding the careers of artists and songwriters, giving them tools and assistance to help them reach a larger audience. Publishers manage the rights to songs and compositions, which include licensing, royalty collection, and distribution. They collaborate closely with composers to market their music to other artists, producers, and media outlets, resulting in placements in films, television series, advertisements, and other projects. Publishers also preserve songwriters' intellectual property rights and ensure they receive fair compensation for their efforts.

Distributors are in charge of providing music to shops, streaming platforms, and other locations where customers may access and purchase music. They collaborate with record labels and artists to distribute physical albums, digital downloads, and streaming releases. Distributors play an important role in making music available to customers throughout the world, allowing artists and composers to contact their fans no matter where they are. Managers are persons or corporations who supervise the careers of musicians and songwriters, offering advice, assistance, and representation.

Managers oversee several elements of an artist's career, such as arranging gigs, negotiating contracts, handling cash, and marketing their music. They act as advocates for artists and songwriters, guiding them through the complexity of the music industry and making smart decisions to improve their careers. Furthermore, producers manage the recording and production of music, collaborating closely with performers and composers to create the intended sound and style. Producers provide technical skill, creative vision, and musical understanding to the recording process, assisting artists and songwriters in achieving their artistic goals and creating polished and professional recordings.

Performing rights organizations (PROs) collect and distribute payments to composers and publishers for public performances of their music. PROs monitor the usage of music in a variety of settings, including radio stations, television networks, live performances, and streaming platforms, and collect royalties for composers and publishers. They serve an important role in ensuring that songwriters receive appropriate compensation for the use of their music.

Understanding the roles and actors in the music industry enables aspiring songwriters to carefully manage their careers and form important connections with key stakeholders. Recognizing each entity's contributions and duties allows songwriters to use these connections to enhance their careers, obtain possibilities for cooperation and promotion, and eventually fulfill their professional goals.

Remaining current on industry trends, advances, and possibilities is critical for aspiring songwriters to flourish in the ever-changing music industry. Staying current on changes in technology, consumer behavior, and market dynamics, songwriters may adjust their strategy, capitalize on new possibilities, and stay ahead of the curve in an increasingly competitive business.

Understanding Copyrights and Royalties

Aspiring composers must grasp copyrights and royalties before beginning their musical careers. These ideas guide how songwriters safeguard their creative works, make money from their songs, and negotiate the complicated environment of the music industry. Copyright is a legal privilege that provides composers with complete ownership over the use and distribution of their original musical works. When a songwriter writes a song, they instantly own the copyright to that work, which gives them the exclusive right to reproduce, distribute, perform, and alter it.

Copyright protection is critical for songwriters because it prevents unlawful use of their music and ensures they receive due credit and recompense for their creative works. Registering your compositions with a performing rights organization (PRO) like ASCAP, BMI, or SESAC is a vital step in protecting your copyright and receiving rewards for public performances of your music.

PROs monitor the usage of music in a variety of settings, including radio stations, television networks, live performances, and streaming platforms, and collect royalties for composers and publishers. Songwriters can earn numerous forms of royalties from their songs. Songwriters receive performance royalties when their songs are publicly performed, whether on the radio, in a live concert, on television, or via streaming services.

Mechanical royalties are paid when music is duplicated and disseminated, such as on physical CDs, digital downloads, or streaming services. Visual media such as films, TV shows, commercials, or video games collect synchronization royalties when they use a song.

Composers can earn money through synchronization licenses, which permit the use of their music in visual media, and performance licenses, which allow their music to be performed in public. Songwriters who want to optimize their revenue potential and guarantee fair compensation for their creative works must understand the various forms of royalties and licensing.

Understanding the complexities of music publishing is required for composers to efficiently manage their copyrights and income. Music publishers promote, license, and administer song and composition rights on behalf of songwriters. They work closely with PROs to collect royalties, arrange licensing deals, and defend composers' intellectual property rights.

Exploring Music Publishing and Licensing

Exploring music publishing and licensing Music publishing and licensing are critical parts of the music industry that songwriters must grasp in order to properly manage their careers and maximize their earnings potential. Music publication is the administration of rights to songs and compositions, whereas licensing is the granting of licenses to utilize music in various mediums and platforms.

Music publishers play an important role in the music industry by representing songwriters and composers and managing their rights to their musical compositions. Publishers market and exploit songs to create money in a variety of ways, including licensing for use in films, TV shows, advertisements, video games, and other media, as well as live performances, digital downloads, and streaming services. Music publishers offer songwriters exclusive rights to exploit their songs and compositions in exchange for a share of the generated revenue. Performing rights organizations (PROs) such as ASCAP, BMI, and SESAC collaborate with music publishers to collect royalties for public song performances and ensure fair compensation for songwriters.

Music publishers not only promote and license songs but also handle the administrative parts of music publishing, such as copyright registration, royalty collection, and accounting. They seek to guarantee that composers get correct and timely royalties for the use of their music while also protecting their intellectual property rights. Songwriters must also understand licensing, which is a crucial component of music publication. Licensing entails granting permission to use music in a variety of contexts, including synchronization licenses for use in visual media such as films, television shows, and commercials, as well as mechanical licenses for music reproduction and distribution on physical media, digital downloads, and streaming platforms.

Songwriters and music publishers negotiate license agreements with corporations and people that want to use their music, establishing the terms and conditions of use, such as length, territory, and pay. Licensing agreements may include the payment of upfront fees or royalties, depending on the use of music. Furthermore, understanding the various forms of license agreements and the rights they entail is critical for songwriters to efficiently manage their music publishing and licensing operations. This involves comprehending the distinction between exclusive and non-exclusive licenses, as well as the rights provided by each type of license, such as the ability to reproduce, distribute, perform, and alter the music.

Learning about music publishing and licensing is critical for budding songwriters who want to successfully manage their careers and optimize their earnings. Understanding the function of music publishers, the licensing process, and the many types of licensing agreements and rights involved allows songwriters to safeguard their creative works, negotiate advantageous terms, and develop successful careers in music.

Building Relationships: Networking in the Industry

Networking is an essential part of beginning a songwriting career and navigating the music industry. Building relationships with other artists, industry experts, and music aficionados may lead to opportunities, collaborations, and mentoring, all of which contribute to a songwriter's career success and longevity. Networking helps songwriters connect with others who share their enthusiasm for music and creativity.

Attending industry events, conferences, seminars, and showcases allows songwriters to meet and engage with other artists, producers, managers, publishers, and industry experts. These conversations give a great opportunity to discuss ideas, share experiences, and form meaningful relationships, which may lead to future collaborations and partnerships.

Networking exposes songwriters to many ideas, styles, and genres in the music industry. By collaborating with a wide group of artists and industry experts, songwriters may extend their horizons, develop their musical vocabulary, and explore new creative opportunities. Networking allows songwriters to learn from others, get inspiration, and push the limits of their creativity. Furthermore, networking provides easy access to significant resources and possibilities for growth and development. By developing ties with industry experts, songwriters may have access to mentoring, direction, and support from seasoned individuals who can provide essential insights and assistance in navigating the music industry landscape.

Networking also opens up options for collaboration, promotion, and exposure, such as co-writing sessions, showcase performances, and music placement in films, television programs, advertisements, and other media. Collaboration is an essential part of networking in the music business. By working with other musicians, songwriters, producers, and industry experts, songwriters may explore new creative avenues, learn from others, and create music that appeals to a larger audience. Collaborations enable songwriters to combine their distinct abilities, skills, and views to produce music that is larger than its parts, resulting in mutual success and progress.

In addition to establishing contacts with other artists and industry professionals, networking entails interacting with music aficionados and fans. Engaging with fans via social media, live concerts, and other platforms enables songwriters to cultivate a dedicated fan base, foster a sense of community around their music, and garner support for their professional goals. Fans may serve as ambassadors for a songwriter's music, spreading the word and helping to expand their audience and reach.

Songwriters who want to start a successful music career must create partnerships through networking. By networking with other artists, industry experts, and music fans, songwriters may obtain vital insights, chances, and support for their careers. Networking enables songwriters to broaden their horizons, collaborate with others, and produce music that appeals to a larger audience, thus contributing to their success and progress in the music industry.

Resources for Songwriters: Organizations and Tools

Songwriters looking to start a career in songwriting have access to a wealth of resources, including organizations and programs geared to help them with their creative aspirations and professional growth. These sites provide essential chances for education, networking, cooperation, promotion, and growth, allowing songwriters to better navigate the music industry environment and achieve their objectives.

Membership-based groups that promote and advocate for songwriters' rights and interests are an important resource for them. These organizations, such as the Songwriters Association of Canada

(SAC), the Nashville Songwriters Association International (NSAI), and the Songwriters Guild of America (SGA), offer their members a variety of benefits, including educational resources, networking opportunities, workshops, mentorship programs, and legal assistance.

Membership in these organizations allows aspiring songwriters to network with other songwriters, learn from industry pros, and remain current on industry trends and advances. Songwriters can also benefit from internet networks and forums, which provide opportunities for collaboration, feedback, and support. Websites like Songwriting Reddit, Songwriters Forum, and Songwriter Universe provide venues for songwriters to discuss their work, exchange ideas, and interact with other songwriters from all around the world.

These online forums offer excellent chances for networking, collaboration, and peer-to-peer learning, allowing songwriters to obtain feedback on their work, cooperate on projects, and develop as artists. In addition to organizations and online groups, songwriters have access to a number of tools and software meant to help them produce songs and improve their creative workflow.

Digital audio workstations (DAWs) like Logic Pro, Pro capabilities, Ableton Live, and GarageBand provide sophisticated recording, arranging, and production capabilities, allowing composers to easily bring their musical ideas to life. Virtual instruments and sample libraries provide composers with a diverse choice of sounds and textures to play with, while music notation software like Sibelius and Finale allows them to precisely notate their compositions and arrangements. Additionally, songwriters can use internet platforms and services for songwriting collaboration, marketing, and distribution.

Websites like SoundBetter, Splice, and Kompoz let songwriters locate partners, hire session musicians, and access professional recording and production services. Streaming platforms like Spotify, Apple Music, and YouTube allow songwriters to promote and distribute their music to a global audience, whereas digital distribution services like DistroKid, TuneCore, and CD Baby allow songwriters to release their music across multiple platforms and collect royalties on streams and downloads.

Budding songwriters have access to a multitude of resources, such as organizations, online forums, and tools, that will help them with their creative aspirations and professional growth. Using these services, songwriters may connect with other songwriters, learn from industry pros, collaborate on projects, market their songs, and better navigate the music industry environment. Whether through membership-based organizations, online forums, or digital tools and services, aspiring songwriters may find the support and resources they need to launch a successful songwriting career.

Crafting Your Professional Identity

Crafting Your Professional Identity Starting a songwriting career entails more than simply composing amazing songs; you must also develop a professional identity that represents your own voice, style, and brand as a songwriter. Your professional identity, encompassing your artistic vision, values, and image, significantly influences how you are perceived within the music business and by your audience.

One of the first stages in developing your professional identity is to define your artistic vision and values as a composer. What topics, sentiments, and feelings do you hope to express through your music? What distinguishes you from other songwriters? Understanding your artistic vision and principles enables you to produce music that is honest and true to yourself, connecting with your audience on a deeper level.

Additionally, your professional identity includes your image and brand as a songwriter. This encompasses both your visual aesthetic (logo, album artwork, and promotional pictures) and your online presence (website, social media profiles, and press kit). Your image and brand should represent your artistic vision and beliefs, sending a clear statement and identity to your target audience and industry experts.

Creating a professional identity entails establishing a strong online presence and digital imprint. In today's digital age, having a website and an active presence on social media sites like Instagram, Twitter, Facebook, and YouTube is critical for reaching and connecting with your target audience. Your web presence should promote your music, communicate your narrative as a songwriter, and allow fans and industry professionals to interact. Furthermore, networking is vital to developing your professional identity as a songwriter. Building relationships with other artists, industry experts, and music aficionados provides you with vital insights, chances, and support for your career.

Networking gives chances for cooperation, marketing, and exposure, allowing you to expand your audience and advance your songwriting career. In addition, developing your professional identity entails sharpening your abilities and always evolving as a songwriter. This involves consistently practicing your art, soliciting feedback and constructive criticism from peers and industry professionals, and attending workshops, seminars, and conferences to broaden your knowledge and abilities. Investing in your professional development as a songwriter will allow you to improve your professional identity and stand out in a competitive business.

Maintaining professionalism throughout your career is critical for developing a solid professional identity. This involves being prompt, dependable, and courteous in encounters with industry professionals, partners, and fans. It also entails behaving with integrity, honesty, and transparency in your commercial transactions and creative activities, therefore winning the confidence and respect of those with whom you collaborate.

Cultivating your professional identity as a composer entails identifying your creative vision and beliefs, creating a strong brand and image, establishing a powerful web presence, successfully networking, polishing your abilities, and being professional in all parts of your business. By devoting time and effort to developing your professional identity, you may position yourself as a renowned and recognizable musician, paving the way for a successful and rewarding songwriting career.

Defining Your Artistic Brand

Defining your artistic identity is one of the most important steps to take while starting a songwriting career. Your artistic identity captures the essence of who you are as a composer and distinguishes you from others in the business. It represents your individual style, voice, beliefs, and the entire experience you provide to your audience. To develop your artistic brand, you must first have a thorough awareness of your musical identity. This entails delving into your musical influences, inspirations, and topics that speak to you personally. Consider the feelings you want to provoke with your music and the message you want to send to your audience.

Understanding your musical identity allows you to begin shaping your artistic brand in a way that is true to you as a songwriter. Once you have a firm understanding of your musical identity, you can begin to establish the major components of your creative brand. This contains details like your musical style, genre, and tone. Consider the musical genres that best express your style and the qualities that distinguish your sound. Whether you like pop, rock, folk, hip-hop, or another genre, your creative identity should represent your musical style and the sound attributes that distinguish your work.

In addition to your musical style, your creative identity includes your lyrical topics, narrative, and the ideas delivered via your songs. Consider the themes and issues that are important to you and that you wish to explore through your music. Whether it's love, heartache, empowerment, social justice, or personal growth, your lyrical themes help shape your artistic brand and connect with your audience on a deeper level.

Your artistic brand encompasses not just your music but also your visual identity and aesthetic. Consider things like your logo, record artwork, advertising images, and merchandising design. Your visual identity should complement your musical style and lyrical ideas, resulting in a unified and memorable brand that connects with your target audience. Take note of the colors, typefaces, and artwork that best reflect your artistic vision and personality as a composer.

Your creative brand encompasses your online presence and how you interact with your audience via digital platforms and social media. Your website, social media profiles, and digital material should represent your artistic identity and allow followers to interact with you. Consider the tone, language, and message you employ in your online communications to ensure they are consistent with your creative identity and successfully communicate your personality and beliefs as a composer. Furthermore, developing your artistic identity entails identifying your unique selling proposition (USP), or what distinguishes you from other composers in the field.

This might be your unique singing style, compositional approach, live performance intensity, or the story behind your music. Identifying your unique selling point allows you to stand out in a competitive market and develop a dedicated fan following that appreciates your unique qualities as a songwriter.

Identifying your artistic brand is an important stage in launching a songwriting career. It entails discovering your musical identity, identifying crucial characteristics such as your musical style, lyrical topics, and visual identity, and developing your unique selling point. Crafting a unified and authentic creative brand allows you to successfully convey your identity as a composer and connect with your audience in a meaningful way, laying the groundwork for a successful and rewarding career in music.

Creating a Compelling Artist Persona

As you begin your road to pursuing a songwriting career, developing a captivating artist persona is critical for establishing your identity in the music industry and engaging with your audience. Your artist persona is the image, personality, and public perception you present as a composer, and it has a significant impact on how fans, industry professionals, and the media perceive you. To develop a captivating artist character, first identify the key elements that distinguish you as a songwriter.

This encompasses your musical style, lyrics, voice delivery, and overall appearance. Reflect on what sets you apart from other composers and how you aspire to be perceived by your audience. Your artist persona should accurately reflect your personality, beliefs, and creative vision, connecting with your audience on a personal basis. Your artist persona is more than just your music; it includes your complete image and public presentation. This covers things like your stage appearance, dress taste, and visual branding. Think about the image you want to project as a songwriter and how you want your audience to remember you.

Your artist persona should reflect who you are as a musician and have an impact on your audience, whether you're known for your edgy style, captivating stage presence, or thought-provoking lyrics. Developing a captivating artist identity necessitates a robust and regular internet presence. This involves keeping active social media profiles on Instagram, Twitter, Facebook, and TikTok, as well as connecting with your audience via digital material like music videos, behind-the-scenes footage, and live streaming.

Your internet presence should reflect your artist identity and allow fans to engage with you on a more personal level, building a sense of community and commitment to your music. Furthermore, developing an engaging artist identity necessitates strong narrative and communication abilities. Your artist persona should be more than simply a visual representation; it should convey a story and elicit emotions in your audience. Whether through music, social media postings, or interviews, properly articulating your narrative as a composer and sharing your experiences, ideas, and goals helps your audience connect with you on a deeper level and engage in your artistic journey.

Developing a captivating artist identity requires staying true to yourself and being real in all parts of your business. Your artist persona should be a true expression of who you are as a composer, and it should evolve naturally as you mature as an artist. Avoid conforming to industry trends or shaping yourself into an image that does not reflect your actual nature. Accept your unique idiosyncrasies, shortcomings, and weaknesses because these are what set you apart and help you connect with your audience on a human level.

Designing Your Online Presence: Website and Social Media

Key factors mentioned while creating your online presence through your website and social media channels:

1. Website Design: Your website is the focal point of your online presence, functioning as a professional portfolio where visitors can discover more about you and your music. Designing a user-friendly website entails establishing an accessible navigation menu, adding high-quality images like pictures and album artwork, and ensuring mobile responsiveness for seamless browsing across several platforms.

2. Content and Sections: Your website should have sections about your music, biography, forthcoming events, and goods. This information gives visitors a thorough overview of your musical path,

allowing them to listen to your music, learn more about your history, and keep up with your most recent albums and performances.

3. Engagement Tools: Include social media links and email subscription forms on your website to encourage users to follow you on other platforms and keep up with your music. Consider creating a press kit area with downloadable content for media professionals and industry contacts.

4. Social Media Strategy: Social media platforms are effective tools for growing and engaging your fan base. Choose channels that are relevant to your intended audience, and focus on providing consistent, interesting material that reflects your personality and musical character.

5. Content Strategy: Stick to a regular publishing schedule on social media to keep your audience interested and develop momentum for your music. Use hashtags wisely to increase your reach, and use multimedia content like photographs, videos, and audio samples to successfully promote your music.

6. Engagement and Collaboration: Connect with your audience by swiftly replying to comments, messages, and mentions, building a sense of community surrounding your music. Collaborate with other artists, influencers, and companies in your field to broaden your reach and attract new fans.7. **Analytics and Optimization**: Use

social media analytics tools to monitor your performance, spot patterns, and optimize your content plan for optimum effect. By examining data such as engagement metrics and audience demographics, you can improve your approach and connect with your target audience.

Promotional Strategies for Independent Songwriters

As an independent composer starting out in the music industry, efficient promotional methods are critical for getting attention, creating a fan base, and finally reaching success.

Here are some extensive, engaging, and complete promotional techniques designed for independent songwriters:

1. Use social media platforms: social media platforms like Instagram, Facebook, Twitter, and TikTok provide great tools for marketing music. Create compelling material that reflects your personality, musical style, and behind-the-scenes experiences. To keep your audience involved and informed, give information on new music releases, future events, and the creative process on a regular basis.

2. Engage with Your Audience: Create a feeling of community by actively connecting with your audience on social media platforms.

Respond to comments, emails, and mentions immediately, and make an effort to interact with your followers on a human level. Hosting live Q&A sessions, freebies, and special content for your fans will help you build stronger relationships with them and boost their commitment to your music.

3. Collaborate with Other Artists: Working with other independent artists, bands, or producers can help you broaden your audience and offer your music to new people. Consider working together on singles, EPs, or music videos, and cross-promote each other's work through social media and other promotional avenues. Collaborations not only expose your music to new audiences, but they also give essential networking chances in the music business.

4. Send Your Music to Music Blogs and Playlists: Look for music blogs, online publications, and playlists that showcase indie performers in your genre. After submitting your music for consideration, maximize your chances of being included by following up with individualized pitches. Having your music published on renowned blogs and playlists might help you gain more attention and attract new listeners.

5. Perform Live and Tour: Live performances are an excellent method to interact with your audience and show off your music in a concrete way. Book shows in small venues, coffee shops, and music festivals to reach new audiences and cultivate a devoted fan base.

Consider creating your own gigs or tours to promote your music in other towns and areas, as well as using social media to inform your followers about forthcoming performances.

6. Create Engaging Visual Content: In addition to your music, visual content like music videos, lyric videos, and behind-the-scenes footage may help capture your audience and boost your promotional efforts. Invest in high-quality images that match your music and convey your artistic concept. Share your visual material on social media and streaming channels to reach new listeners and keep existing fans engaged.

7. Create an Email List: Email marketing is still one of the most successful methods to engage with your audience and promote your music. Encourage fans to subscribe to your email list via your website and social media platforms, and send them newsletters on a regular basis with information on your music, forthcoming events, and special content. Personalize your emails so that your fans feel valued and involved with your music.

8. Network and Collaborate with Industry Professionals: Connecting with industry professionals such as producers, managers, booking agents, and music supervisors can lead to new possibilities and partnerships. Attend music industry events, conferences, and networking mixers to meet local industry people and develop ties that can help you succeed in your music career.

9. Offer Merchandise and Limited Edition Releases: Utilize merchandise such as t-shirts, posters, and vinyl records to generate additional cash and promote your music. Create goods that express your brand identity and connect with your fans, and sell them at your live concerts and online store. Consider producing limited-edition tangible versions of your music, such as vinyl records or cassette tapes, to generate excitement and exclusivity for your releases.

10. Use the Power of Online Streaming Platforms: Use internet streaming services like Spotify, Apple Music, and YouTube to promote your music and reach a worldwide audience. Create artist profiles on these sites, optimize them with engaging imagery and interesting artist bios, and consistently release new music to keep your audience interested. Collaborate with playlist curators and influencers to get your music published on prominent playlists and channels, and promote it to your social media and email subscribers.

Collaborating with Other Artists and Producers

Collaboration with other musicians and producers is an effective technique for songwriters seeking to launch their careers in the music industry. These collaborations allow you to broaden your network, boost your creativity, and reach new audiences.

Here's a thorough look into cooperating with different artists and producers:

When working with other artists, you may combine your distinct abilities and views to create something better than the sum of its parts. Collaboration, whether with other composers, instrumentalists, vocalists, or producers, helps you tap into a variety of creative impulses and methods, resulting in dynamic and multidimensional music.

Collaborating with other songwriters can bring new insights and ideas that can inspire your own composing process. Sharing songwriting tasks allows you to experiment with different song structures, melodies, and lyrics, resulting in more rich and diversified songs. Working with vocalists allows you to experiment with harmonies, vocal arrangements, and duets, which adds depth and character to your songs. Instrumental collaborations allow you to explore new musical landscapes and genres.

Working with experienced instrumentalists may improve your work by using complicated melodies, solos, and arrangements that highlight their abilities. Collaborating with producers allows you to benefit from their technical knowledge and production expertise, which improves the quality and polish of your recordings.

Collaborations can provide excellent networking opportunities in the music business. Working with other artists and producers allows you to leverage their networks of contacts, which include industry experts, labels, and music supervisors. These relationships may lead to new chances, such as live performances, music licensing agreements, and placements in film, television, and advertising.

Working with other musicians and producers promotes a sense of community and mutual support within the music industry. It enables you to form relationships with like-minded creatives who share your enthusiasm for music, potentially leading to long-term collaborations and creative partnerships. These partnerships may offer emotional support, feedback, and encouragement as you progress through your songwriting journey. Partnering with other musicians and producers is an effective method for songwriters starting out in the music industry. It allows you to express your creativity, reach new audiences, and develop partnerships within the music community.

Recording and Producing Your Music

Recording and producing your own music is an important part of establishing a songwriting career since it allows you to bring your musical ideas to life and share them with the world. Whether you're recording demos in your bedroom or working in a professional recording studio, the process of recording and creating music entails numerous important processes and considerations.

First and foremost, you must have a clear vision of the sound you wish to produce with your music. This involves determining the instruments, arrangement, and general mood of your music. Whether you want a stripped-down acoustic sound or a fully polished pop composition, having a clear vision can help guide your recording and production efforts.

Next, think about the tools and software you'll need for recording and creating your song. This can include everything from basic recording equipment like microphones, audio interfaces, and headphones to more complex equipment like studio monitors, MIDI controllers, and digital audio workstations (DAWs). Choose equipment and software that are appropriate for your budget, technical ability level, and desired degree of production quality.

Once you've set up your equipment, it's time to start recording music. This entails recording your songs' performances, whether that's using live instruments, MIDI sequences, or vocal tracks. To achieve high-quality recordings, consider microphone location, room acoustics, and signal flow. During the recording process, don't be scared to experiment and try new ways to get the sound you want. This might include layering many tracks, utilizing effects and processing techniques, or inserting unusual instruments or noises into your recordings.

The recording procedure allows you to unleash your creativity and find new methods to communicate your musical thoughts. Once you've recorded all of the individual tracks for your songs, you may go on to the production process. This includes editing, arranging, and mixing your recordings to produce a coherent and polished finished product. Use your DAW's editing tools to remove any faults or defects in the recordings, organize the tracks in a logical and dynamic order, and apply effects and processing to improve the overall sound.

Mixing and Mastering Your Tracks

Mixing is an important phase in the production process since it involves balancing the levels of different tracks, changing the frequency balance, and adding effects like reverb, delay, and compression to create depth and dimension in your mix. Take the time to listen attentively to your mix on various playback systems and make any necessary tweaks to get professional-quality sound.

Mastering is the final phase in the production process, and it entails preparing the final mix for distribution by improving overall sound quality, altering volume levels, and maintaining uniformity across all songs. Hire a professional mastering engineer or use mastering software to get the finest results.

However, while you traverse the recording and production process, it's important to keep a few other concerns in mind:

1. **Budget and Resources:** Set a budget for recording and producing your music, including the cost of equipment, studio time (if applicable), software, and any professional services you may require, such as mixing and mastering. Consider investigating low-cost possibilities, such as home recording setups or collaborating with other artists who have access to recording equipment.

2. Technical Skills and Learning Curve: Be prepared to spend time learning how to utilize your recording equipment and software successfully. There may be a learning curve, particularly if you are unfamiliar with recording and producing procedures. Make use of online tutorials, workshops, and courses to improve your technical abilities and expertise.

3. Collaboration and Outsourcing: Don't be afraid to work with other musicians, producers, or engineers who may have greater experience or expertise in recording and producing. Working with professionals may improve the quality of your recordings while also providing useful insights and criticism on your music. Consider outsourcing chores like mixing and mastering to experienced specialists if you believe it is required to attain the appropriate level of quality.

4. Creativity and Experimentation: Encourage creativity and experimentation throughout the recording and production process. Don't be hesitant to try out new recording techniques, experiment with different sounds and effects, and push the limits of your musical style. The recording studio is a creative playground where you can try out fresh ideas and techniques for bringing your music to life.

5. Feedback and Revision: Seek input from trustworthy peers, mentors, or industry pros throughout the recording and production process. Their feedback can give you useful information and help you find areas for development. Be willing to revise and improve your recordings based on comments, since this may lead to a better finished result.

6. Persistence and Patience: Recording and producing music may be a time-consuming and difficult task, especially if you want professional-quality results. Be prepared to dedicate time and effort to each phase of the process, and do not let failures or roadblocks along the way discourage you. Maintain your persistence and patience, and remember that each recording session and production assignment is an opportunity to learn and improve as a musician and composer.

Setting Up a Home Studio on a Budget

Aspiring songwriters can get started in the music industry without breaking the bank by setting up a low-cost home studio. With technological improvements and cheap recording equipment, it is now simpler than ever to produce high-quality recordings from the comfort of your own home.

Here's a thorough look at how to set up a home studio on a budget:

1. Select the Right Space: The first step in establishing a home studio is to choose the appropriate location. Look for a room that is peaceful and well-ventilated, with enough space to house your recording equipment and instruments. Consider things like natural lighting, acoustics, and closeness to power outlets.

2. Essential Equipment: Invest in recording equipment that is within your budget. Consider using a dependable audio interface with several inputs and outputs to connect microphones, instruments, and monitors.

Microphones: Look for adaptable microphones that can capture vocalists, acoustic instruments, and amplifiers. Consider using a dynamic microphone for vocalists and a large-diaphragm condenser microphone for recording acoustic instruments.

Studio Monitors or Headphones: Invest in a set of studio monitors or high-quality headphones to ensure proper monitoring of your recordings. Look for alternatives with a flat frequency response and a clear stereo image.

Digital Audio Workstation (DAW): Select a DAW that matches your workflow and budget. Many DAWs provide cheap choices for novices, including multitrack recording, MIDI sequencing, and audio editing.

MIDI Controller: Consider including a MIDI controller keyboard in your setup for programming virtual instruments and generating MIDI sequences.

3. Acoustic Treatment: Improving the acoustics in your home studio can improve the sound quality of your recordings. To reduce unwanted reflections and increase sound clarity, consider using low-cost acoustic treatment alternatives such as foam panels, bass traps, and diffusers.

4. DIY Solutions: To save money, consider DIY equipment and acoustic treatment options. For example, you may make your own microphone isolation shield out of PVC pipes and acoustic foam, as well as DIY bass traps out of fiberglass insulation and cloth.

5. Software and Plugins: Use free or low-cost software and plugins to improve your recordings. Many DAWs include built-in effects and virtual instruments, and free plugins let you add effects like reverb, delay, EQ, and compression to your recordings.

6. Optimize Your Process: Organize your home studio process to increase efficiency and productivity. Organize your equipment and cords for simple access, use your DAW to build templates and presets for common recording and mixing jobs, and develop a maintenance and organizing routine for your studio.

7. Continual Learning and Improvement: Make time to study and improve your recording and producing talents. Use online tutorials, forums, and courses to improve your understanding of recording techniques, audio engineering ideas, and music production concepts.

8. Collaborate and Network: Work with other artists, producers, and engineers to acquire experience and build your network. Participate in online communities, forums, and social media groups to meet like-minded people and share your music. To summarize, setting up a home studio on a budget is an attainable objective for young songwriters hoping to launch their music careers.

You can create high-quality recordings and lay the groundwork for a successful songwriting career by investing in necessary recording equipment, improving the acoustics of your space, exploring DIY solutions, leveraging free or affordable software and plugins, optimizing your workflow, constantly learning and improving your skills, and collaborating and networking with others in the music community.

Basics of Audio Recording and Production

As an aspiring songwriter trying to launch a music career, learning the fundamentals of audio recording and production is critical for producing high-quality recordings of your compositions. Audio recording and production entails capturing, editing, and mixing audio to produce polished and professional-sounding songs.

Here's a thorough look at the fundamentals of audio recording and production:

1. **Sound Waves and Signal Flow:** Sound waves are movements in the air that microphones detect as electrical impulses. Understanding the basics of sound waves and signal flow is essential for audio recording. In a conventional recording setup, microphones catch sound waves, transform them into electrical signals, and then process and modify them using various audio equipment.
2. **Microphones:** Microphones are devices that record sound waves and convert them to electrical impulses. There are various varieties of microphones, including dynamic, condenser, and ribbon microphones, each having unique properties and applications. Dynamic microphones are durable and adaptable, making them ideal for recording vocals and instruments. Condenser mics are more sensitive and catch more detail, so they are perfect for recording voices and acoustic

instruments with more clarity and fidelity. Ribbon microphones produce smooth, natural sound, making them ideal for recording voices, strings, and brass instruments.

3. **Audio Interfaces:** An audio interface is a device that links microphones, instruments, and other audio equipment to a computer to allow for audio recording and processing. An audio interface converts analog audio signals into digital data that can be recorded and processed using digital audio workstation (DAW) software. Audio interfaces provide a variety of inputs and outputs to support diverse recording settings, ranging from single-channel interfaces for solo recording to multi-channel interfaces for recording numerous sources at once.

4. **Digital Audio Workstations (DAWs):** A digital audio workstation (DAW) is software that allows you to record, edit, and mix audio files. DAWs create a virtual studio environment in which you can record numerous tracks, edit audio clips, apply effects and processing, and combine your recordings into a final mix. Popular DAWs include Pro Tools, Logic Pro, Ableton Live, FL Studio, and Reaper, each having their own unique set of capabilities and workflows.

5. **Recording Techniques:** Understanding fundamental recording techniques is critical for producing high-quality recordings. This includes microphone positioning, which affects the sound quality and stereo image of the recorded signal. Experimenting

with different microphone locations, such as close-miking, room miking, and stereo miking approaches, can help you obtain the sound you want for different instruments and vocalists.

6. **Editing and Processing:** Editing and processing audio entails modifying recorded audio fragments to produce the desired sound. This involves duties like editing and chopping audio clips, altering volume levels, and using equalization (EQ), compression, reverb, delay, and other effects to improve the sound quality and melody of the recordings. Understanding how to use your DAW's editing and processing tools is critical to defining the overall sound of your recordings.

7. **Mixing:** Mixing is the process of mixing various audio files to create a smooth and balanced final mix. To get a clean and dynamic sound, alter each track's volume levels, panning placements, and frequency balance. Mixing also includes adding effects like reverb, delay, and modulation to provide depth and dimension in the mix. Learning how to use mixing tools like faders, EQ, compression, and effects in your DAW is critical for producing professional-sounding mixes.

8. **Mastering:** The final phase in the audio production process is to produce the final mix for distribution. This is adding finishing touches to the mix, such as adjusting the overall volume level, applying final EQ and compression, and ensuring consistency

and balance throughout all songs. Mastering also includes preparing the final mix for distribution by encoding it into several audio formats and adding metadata like track names, album artwork, and ISRC codes.

Working with Session Musicians and Producers

Working with session musicians and producers is an important part of launching a songwriting career since it helps you to improve the quality and inventiveness of your music while also developing your network in the music business. Session musicians are hired to play on recordings or during live performances, while producers oversee the recording and production process to achieve the desired sound for a single or album.

Collaboration with session musicians has various advantages for songwriters. To begin, session musicians add a high degree of knowledge and proficiency to your recordings, improving the overall quality of your music. They may add depth, texture, and musicality to your songs through instrumental or vocal performances, improving the overall sound and impact of your creations.

Furthermore, session musicians may inject new ideas and views into your music, providing creative feedback and recommendations that may spark new paths or arrangements for your tunes.

When working with session musicians, you must explain your vision and goals effectively. Provide them with sheet music, chord charts, or audio demonstrations of your compositions, as well as any special instructions or preferences for the music's style, feel, and arrangement. Be receptive to their comments and critiques, since they might improve the musicianship and inventiveness of your works. Collaboration with producers is another excellent chance for songwriters wishing to launch their careers in music. Producers are skilled individuals who manage the recording, arrangement, and production of songs or albums, leading the creative process to create the intended aural vision for the music.

They collaborate closely with songwriters to bring their musical ideas to life, providing technical experience, creative input, and invaluable advice throughout the recording and production process. Working with a producer may greatly assist songwriters in improving their musical ideas, developing their tone, and creating professional-quality recordings. Producers bring a plethora of expertise and knowledge to the table, providing perspectives on song arrangement, instrumentation, vocal performance, and sound aesthetics.

They may also give helpful critiques and recommendations for increasing the overall quality and impact of your music, allowing you to realize your full creative potential as a songwriter. When working with producers, it is critical to have open communication and a collaborative working environment.

Discuss your creative vision, project goals, and expectations, as well as any specific ideas or preferences you have for the musical tone and style. Be receptive to their innovative recommendations and feedback, as they may provide useful insights and ideas to improve the quality and inventiveness of your music.

Distributing Your Music: Digital Platforms and Physical Releases

Distributing your music is an important step in launching a songwriting career since it helps you reach a larger audience and establish a fan base.

In today's digital era, you may distribute your music through a variety of channels and ways, including digital and physical releases:

1. Digital Distribution Platforms: Digital distribution platforms have transformed the music industry by enabling independent musicians to release and distribute their work globally. These platforms let you post your music and make it available for streaming and downloading through a variety of online retailers and streaming services.

Some popular digital distribution platforms include:

Spotify: One of the most popular streaming services, Spotify allows you to publish your music via a digital distributor and reach millions of listeners worldwide. Apple Music: Apple Music is another popular streaming service that allows you to release your music through digital distributors such as TuneCore and DistroKid.

Amazon Music: Amazon Music provides digital distribution services for independent musicians, enabling them to access fans via Amazon's online shop and streaming service.

Bandcamp: Bandcamp is a popular website that allows independent musicians to sell and distribute their music directly to listeners. It provides price freedom and allows you to retain a greater portion of your sales income.

2. Digital Distribution Services: In addition to digital distribution platforms, there are digital distribution services that allow you to release your music to a variety of online retailers and streaming services. These firms operate as go-betweens for you and digital platforms, managing the technical aspects of distribution and ensuring that your music reaches a large audience.

Some popular digital distribution services include:

TuneCore: TuneCore is a digital distribution business that assists independent musicians in distributing their music to different online retailers and streaming platforms, such as Spotify, Apple Music, and Amazon.

DistroKid: DistroKid is another digital distribution business that provides an easy and cost-effective way to distribute your music to major online retailers and streaming platforms. It also includes tools for advertising your music, tracking sales, and streaming data.

CD Baby: CD Baby is a digital distribution business that focuses on delivering music to online shops, streaming services, and physical retailers. It provides a variety of distribution channels, including digital, physical, and licensing services.

3. Physical Releases: Although digital distribution has been the major way of distributing music in recent years, physical releases remain valuable to many artists. Physical releases include CDs, vinyl albums, and cassette tapes, providing fans with a tactile and collectible experience.

Physical releases can be disseminated in several ways, including:

Online Stores: You may sell physical copies of your music via online retailers such as Bandcamp, CD Baby, and your own website. These sites let you sell CDs, vinyl albums, and other tangible media directly to fans.

Retail Stores: Physical releases can also be sent to physical retail locations, such as independent record stores, chain stores, and specialized shops. This might entail collaborating with distributors or approaching retail outlets directly to have your music distributed.

Sales: Physical releases can be packed with t-shirts, posters, and other stuff to provide added value to fans and increase sales.

4. Marketing and Promotion: Regardless of the distribution channel you use, marketing and promotion are critical for increasing exposure and drawing listeners to your music. Use social media, email newsletters, press releases, and online advertising to promote your music and connect with your audience. Collaborate with influencers, music bloggers, and other artists to reach new audiences and generate buzz for your releases.

Music Publishing Negotiation

While negotiating the process of publishing your music, you should consider the following factors:

1. Rights and Royalties: Before distributing your music digitally, be sure you understand the rights and royalties connected with each platform and service. Digital distribution platforms and services often collect and disburse royalties on your behalf in accordance with the terms of their agreements. Ensure fair compensation for your music by familiarizing yourself with royalty rates, payment schedules, and distribution agreements.

2. Metadata and Tagging: Proper tagging and metadata ensure that your music is correctly categorized and searchable across digital platforms. When uploading your music, be sure to include track titles, artist names, album titles, genres, and release dates. Including

this information enables listeners to discover your music and ensures proper credit for your effort.

3. Streaming vs. Download Sales: When deciding which digital distribution channel to use, weigh the benefits and drawbacks of streaming vs. download sales. Streaming services provide significant visibility and access to a huge audience while often paying smaller royalties per stream. Download sales, on the other hand, pay larger royalties per sale but may have a lower reach than streaming services. Evaluate your objectives and priorities to establish the optimal music distribution plan.

4. tangible distribution expenses: When distributing tangible items like CDs or vinyl records, factor in the expenses of production, packing, and shipping. Calculate production costs and develop a price plan that will allow you to pay your expenditures while remaining competitive in the market. Look into bulk production and fulfillment services to cut expenses and expedite the distribution process.

5. Worldwide Reach: Use digital distribution outlets to reach a worldwide audience with your music. Digital platforms provide global distribution, allowing you to reach listeners in several nations and regions without the use of physical distribution infrastructure. Consider your music's global ramifications and customize your

marketing and promotion activities to appeal to a varied audience throughout the world.

6. Consistency and Quality: To create trust and credibility with your audience, ensure that your music releases are consistent and high-quality. Ensure that you properly record, mix, and master your music to meet industry standards. To keep your audience engaged and interested in your music, release new music on a regular basis and interact with them via social media, live concerts, and other avenues.

7. Feedback and Analytics: Monitor listener feedback and analytics to learn how your music is being received and consumed. Monitor streaming analytics, download sales, social media interaction, and other indications to determine the efficacy of your distribution initiatives. Use this input to fine-tune your marketing and promotion methods and enhance future releases.

Building a Fanbase and Generating Income

Starting a successful songwriting career requires both building a fan following and making revenue. As a composer, your fans are your most precious asset, and building a loyal following is critical for long-term success in the music industry.

Here's a thorough look at how to establish an audience and produce revenue as a songwriter:

Focus on developing engaging content that connects with your target audience. This involves releasing high-quality music, eye-catching images, and compelling narration. Share behind-the-scenes looks into your creative process, engage with your followers on social media, and provide unique material in exchange for their support.

Maintain a steady release schedule to engage and excite audiences about your music. Whether you're releasing singles, EPs, or albums, maintaining a consistent release schedule keeps you relevant in the eyes of your audience and encourages them to stay engaged with your music.

Live performances provide a unique opportunity to engage with and grow your fan base. Live performances, whether tiny acoustic settings, full-band concerts, or virtual live broadcasts, provide you the opportunity to display your music and personality in a unique and unforgettable way.

Create an online presence using social media, streaming services, and your own website to reach a larger audience. Engage with your followers on a regular basis, provide music updates, and join online groups and forums that are relevant to your genre or specialty.

Create and sell branded products, like t-shirts, posters, stickers, and bundles, to increase revenue and enhance fan relationships. To incentivise sales, consider giving apparel bundles with unique goods or supplementary material in addition to your music releases.

Consider using crowdfunding services like Patreon, Kickstarter, or GoFundMe to gain cash and support from your followers. Provide your supporters with special benefits, prizes, and experiences in exchange for their donations, such as access to exclusive material, behind-the-scenes updates, or customized notes.

Explore licensing and synchronization chances for your music in various media projects, including films, TV series, advertisements, and video games. Sync licensing may provide a consistent source of revenue and publicity for your music, as well as possibilities to reach new audiences and grow your fan base.

Collaborating with artists, composers, producers, and brands may help you reach new audiences. Collaborative initiatives, guest appearances, and cross-promotions may introduce your music to new audiences while also providing exciting prospects for expansion and exposure. Develop ties with industry people, such as song publishers, record labels, booking agencies, and music supervisors.

Attend industry events, conferences, and networking mixers to meet possible collaborators and connections who may help you further your career and open up new prospects. To diversify your income streams, consider music licensing, item sales, live performances, streaming royalties, crowdfunding, and fan support. As a songwriter, diversifying your income streams allows you to generate a more consistent and sustainable income.

Engaging with Your Audience: Live Performances and Online Interaction

Engaging with your audience is an important part of launching a successful songwriting career.

Building a solid connection with your audience allows you to nurture a devoted following, form meaningful relationships, and eventually construct a long-term music career. Live performances and online interactions are two effective methods to engage your audience.

Live performances: Live performances provide an unparalleled opportunity to engage with your audience on a personal and emotional level. Live performances, whether an intimate acoustic concert at a local coffee shop or a high-energy event in a music venue, provide you the opportunity to present your music in a dynamic and immersive setting.

Connecting with Your Audience: During live performances, take the time to interact with your audience between songs. Share the story behind your songs, anecdotes from your creative process, or personal events that influenced your music. This not only adds dimension to your presentation but also helps your audience connect with you on a more personal level. Encourage audience involvement and participation in live performances.

This might include asking the audience to sing along, clap their hands, or take part in call-and-response passages. Engaging your audience in this way fosters a sense of camaraderie and community, making the live experience more memorable and pleasurable for all participants.

Create Memorable Moments: During your live performances, aim to generate memorable moments that will make an impression on your audience. This might be a spectacular vocal performance, an enthralling instrumental solo, or an emotional engagement with the audience. These unforgettable moments help you connect with your audience and increase the overall impact of your presentation.

Online interactions: In addition to live performances, online participation is an important technique to connect with your audience and establish a loyal following. With the growth of social media and digital platforms, musicians today have more ways than ever to engage with fans all over the world.

Social media engagement: Use social media channels like Instagram, Facebook, Twitter, and TikTok to interact with your audience on a consistent basis. Share updates on your music, behind-the-scenes looks into your creative process, and personal insights into your life as an artist. Respond to your fans' comments, emails, and mentions to create a sense of community and connection.

Live Q&As and Virtual Events: Hold live Q&A sessions, virtual concerts, or listening parties on platforms such as Instagram Live, Facebook Live, or YouTube Live to communicate with your audience in real time. These interactive events let you answer questions, share experiences, and engage with your followers on a more personal level, even if they live halfway around the world.

Fan Engagement Campaigns: Launch fan engagement programs or challenges to stimulate participation and conversation among your audience. This might include competitions, freebies, or fan-created content challenges in which fans can express their creativity and love for your music.

Personalized communication: Take the time to engage with your supporters on a more personal level, whether through direct messaging, individual answers to comments, or handwritten letters. Expressing genuine gratitude to your followers and appreciating their support goes a long way toward developing a strong and devoted audience.

Connecting with your audience through live performances and online contact is critical for launching a successful songwriting career. Create unforgettable experiences during live concerts, develop community and connection through social media and digital platforms, and engage with your fans on a personal level to establish a large and dedicated fanbase that will support you throughout your musical career.

Strategies for Growing Your Fanbase: Social Media, Email Lists, and Merchandise

Growing your fan base is vital for starting and maintaining a successful songwriting career. To effectively extend your audience, use smart techniques across several platforms and channels.

Here are some thorough ideas for expanding your fan base using social media, email lists, and merchandise:

Social media engagement: Use social media networks like Instagram, Facebook, Twitter, TikTok, and YouTube to engage with your target audience and broaden your reach. Create compelling material that reflects your music, personality, and songwriting journey. Share behind-the-scenes looks at your creative process, live performances, music videos, and personal tales to fascinate your audience and establish a deep relationship.

A Consistent Posting Schedule: Maintain a regular publishing schedule to keep your audience engaged and interested in your material. Consistency is essential for being visible in social media feeds and developing momentum with your audience, whether it's through daily, weekly, or biweekly postings. Interact with Your Audience: Actively participate with your audience by replying to comments, messages, and mentions. Express genuine gratitude for their assistance and spark a conversation that builds a sense of community and connection. Ask questions, solicit input, and include your audience in your creative process to make them feel valued and included.

Collaborate with Other Artists: Work with other artists, musicians, and influencers to reach new audiences and grow your fan base. Cross-promote each other's music, collaborate on songs or cover videos, and take part in joint live broadcasts or events to reach a larger audience and connect with each other's fanbases.

Mailing Lists and Newsletters: Create an email list of devoted admirers who want to be informed about your music, events, and other developments. In exchange for joining your email list, provide incentives such as exclusive material, free downloads, or access to pre-sale tickets. Keep your audience involved and informed by sending out newsletters on a regular basis with updates, announcements, and special offers.

Personalized communication: Personalize your interactions with email list members to make them feel valued and appreciated. Address them by their first name, personalize your material to their interests, and segment your email list based on demographics or preferences to offer targeted and relevant information.

Merchandise and branded products: Create and sell clothing such as t-shirts, caps, posters, stickers, and other branded things with your logo, artwork, or song lyrics. Merchandise not only provides additional revenue, but it also acts as an effective marketing tool for promoting your brand and growing your fan base.

Limited Editions and Exclusive Items: Offer limited edition or exclusive stuff to instill a feeling of urgency and exclusivity among your fans. This might be limited-edition vinyl albums, signed posters, or special retail packages with unreleased music or behind-the-scenes footage.

Merchandise Bundles: Create merchandise bundles that mix many goods into a single package, giving fans more value and a reason to buy. Bundle retail products with digital downloads, concert tickets, or admission to exclusive events to encourage people to support your music and interact with your company.

Monetizing Your Music: Streaming Revenue, Merchandising, and Live Gigs

Monetizing your music is an important part of launching a songwriting career since it allows you to make money from your creative work while also supporting your lifestyle as an artist. You may monetize your music in a variety of ways, including by streaming money, purchasing merchandise, and attending live concerts.

Streaming revenue: In today's digital age, streaming services have emerged as one of musicians' key revenue streams. Users may stream music on-demand through platforms such as Spotify, Apple Music, Amazon Music, and Tidal, which pay artists royalties depending on the number of plays their songs receive. While streaming income per stream is tiny, the cumulative effect of several broadcasts may be significant over time, particularly for successful artists with a large fan following. To optimize your streaming earnings, prioritize expanding your visibility on streaming platforms through strategic playlist positions, partnerships with other artists, and music marketing on social media and other digital platforms.

Merchandising: Merchandising is another profitable option to sell your music while also connecting with your audience on a more physical basis. You may increase your revenue and deepen your engagement with your fans by designing and selling stuff such as t-shirts, caps, posters, vinyl records, and other branded things with your logo, artwork, or song lyrics. Merchandise not only allows fans to show their support for your music, but it also acts as an effective marketing tool for promoting your brand and broadening your audience. To effectively commercialize your music through merchandising, make stuff that speaks to your fandom, market it on your website, social media, and at live events, and provide exclusive or limited edition things to generate a feeling of urgency and exclusivity among your followers.

Live gigs: Live performances and gigs have long been a reliable source of income for artists, allowing them to exhibit their music, interact with their audience, and make money through ticket sales, item sales, and performance fees. Whether you're playing at a local club, a music festival, or a private event, live shows enable you to interact with your fans in a dynamic and immersive atmosphere, producing unforgettable experiences that reinforce their devotion and support for your music. To monetize your music through live concerts, book performances at venues that cater to your target demographic, market your gigs using social media, email lists, and local media outlets, and sell merchandise and other things at your shows to optimize your earnings.

Exploring Opportunities in Sync Licensing and Film/TV Placements

Exploring options in sync licensing and film and TV placements may be a profitable and satisfying path for songwriters wishing to launch their careers. Synchronization licensing allows music to be placed in a variety of media, including films, television shows, advertisements, video games, and other visual material.

Here's a thorough look at how you can get into this sector of the music industry and start your songwriting career:

Understanding Sync Licensing: Sync licensing is the process of syncing audio and visual media. This can involve incorporating a song into a film scene, television show, commercial, video game, or other kind of visual media. Producers or authors of the visual material usually negotiate sync licenses with music publishers, record labels, or individual composers.

Advantages of Sync Licensing: Sync licensing provides various benefits to songwriters. For starters, it exposes your music to a larger audience as viewers of the visual material in which it is embedded hear it. This exposure can result in greater recognition and chances for your music. Second, sync licensing may be a substantial source of income since you receive royalties every time your music is synced with visual material. Finally, having your music used in films, television shows, or advertisements may boost your recognition as a songwriter and lead to other possibilities in the business.

Identifying Sync Licensing Opportunities: As a songwriter, you have various options for finding sync licensing possibilities. One strategy is to collaborate with music libraries and sync companies that specialize in linking composers with possibilities in cinema, television, advertising, and other visual media. These organizations actively seek placements for their song collection and pitch it to producers and creators that require music for their projects. Another method is to network with filmmakers, directors, producers, and music supervisors who work on visual material. Attending industry events, conferences, and film festivals may help you interact with industry people and promote your music.

Prepare Your Music for Sync Licensing: To maximize your chances of getting sync licensing possibilities, make sure your music is well-produced, professionally recorded, and appropriate for the visual medium. This entails paying attention to things like production quality, instrumentation, lyrical substance, and overall mood and ambiance. Consider making instrumental versions or stems of your songs, as they are more adaptable and simpler to use in many sorts of visual material. In addition, ensure that you have all of the essential rights and approvals for your music, including composition (songwriting) and sound recording (master).

Submitting Your Music for Sync Licensing: When presenting your music for sync licensing options, be sure to personalize your pitch to the unique needs and tastes of the project or production you're pursuing. Research the style, tone, and topics of the visual material you're proposing, and choose songs from your library that are appropriate. Consider putting together a professional pitch package that includes high-quality recordings, lyrics, metadata, and any other pertinent information about your song. Personalize your proposals and follow up with industry connections to increase your chances of success.

Developing Relationships in the Industry: Building connections with filmmakers, directors, producers, and music supervisors is essential for unlocking sync licensing opportunities. Be proactive in contacting business people, attending industry events, and taking advantage of networking possibilities. Encourage genuine connections and partnerships with creatives in the film and television industries, since these relationships may lead to profitable sync licensing placements.

Maximizing Revenue Streams: Diversification and Financial Management

Maximizing revenue sources is critical for songwriters trying to launch their careers and survive financially in the music industry. Diversification and efficient financial management are crucial ways to achieve this aim, allowing songwriters to earn money from a variety of sources while maintaining long-term financial security.

Diversified Revenue Streams: Diversifying revenue streams entails producing cash from a variety of sources both within and beyond the music industry. This strategy not only boosts overall earnings, but it also gives stability and resistance to swings in any particular income stream.

Here's how songwriters may diversify their earning streams:

1. Performance Royalties: Performance royalties are earned when your music is publicly aired, such as on radio, TV, live performances, and streaming platforms. Joining a Performing Rights Organization (PRO) such as ASCAP, BMI, or SESAC guarantees that you will earn royalties for public performances of your work.
2. Mechanical royalties: Mechanical royalties are received from the reproduction and distribution of your music, which includes physical CD and vinyl record sales as well as digital

downloads. Songwriters can earn mechanical royalties through organizations like the Harry Fox Agency (HFA) or directly from digital distribution platforms like CD Baby, TuneCore, or DistroKid.

3. **Sync Licensing:** License your music for usage in movies, television, advertisements, video games, and other visual media. This may be a profitable revenue source because it includes upfront sync fees and recurring royalties for each usage of your music in visual material.

4. **Merchandising:** Selling stuff such as t-shirts, caps, posters, vinyl records, and other branded things with your logo, artwork, or lyrics may be a viable revenue source. Merchandising not only creates revenue, but it also develops your brand and fosters a stronger bond with your customers.

5. **Live Performance:** Live concerts and gigs offer opportunities to earn money through ticket sales, merchandise sales, and performance fees. Touring, playing festivals, and scheduling concerts at venues are all methods to monetize your live performances and connect with your audience in important ways.

6. **Digital Sales and Streaming:** Platforms like iTunes, Spotify, Apple Music, Amazon Music, and others allow you to generate cash from digital downloads and streaming of your music. While the revenue per stream may be minimal, the

combined effect of numerous streams might be significant over time.

Financial Management: Effective financial management is essential for songwriters to make sound financial decisions, budget successfully, and prepare for the future.

Here are some important areas of money management for songwriters.

1. Budget: Make a budget outlining your revenue and expenses, including those for music creation, promotion, touring, and living expenses. Tracking your spending helps you manage your cash flow and allocate resources more efficiently.

2. Savings and Investments: Set aside a percentage of your earnings for savings and investments to increase your financial stability and prepare for unforeseen costs. Consider investing in retirement accounts, stocks, bonds, or other investment vehicles to help you build wealth over time.

3. Tax Planning: Understand the tax consequences of your music revenue and use available deductions and credits to reduce your tax bill. Consult a tax consultant or accountant that specializes in dealing with artists to guarantee tax compliance and optimize tax savings.

4. Financial Planning: Create a long-term financial strategy that is in line with your job objectives and desires. This may entail identifying financial objectives, developing a timeframe for reaching them, and evaluating and updating your strategy on a regular basis as needed.

5. Professional Advice: Seek help from music-specific financial specialists such as accountants, financial planners, or business managers. They may offer invaluable advice and experience as you negotiate the challenges of managing your money as a composer.

Sustaining Long-Term Success in Songwriting

Long-term success in songwriting necessitates a combination of originality, tenacity, adaptation, and strategic thinking. As you begin your path to start a songwriting career, it is critical to build habits and techniques that will help you grow and thrive in the music industry.

1. Continuously Improve Your Craft: Successful songwriters are constantly seeking to enhance their art. Set aside time for regular practice, songwriting sessions, and experimenting with various styles, genres, and methods. Seek input from trustworthy peers, mentors, and industry specialists to help you find areas for growth and enhance your abilities.
2. Remain inspired and Creative: Maintaining inspiration and creativity is essential for long-term success in songwriting. Surround yourself with many sources of inspiration, such as music, art, literature, nature, and personal stories. Keep a diary to record ideas, lyrics, melodies, and themes as they occur to you, and make a point of trying new things and stretching your creative bounds.

3. **Create a Strong Support Network:** Creating a solid support network of fellow songwriters, collaborators, mentors, and industry experts is critical for navigating the complexities of a songwriting career. Surround yourself with like-minded people who understand the ups and downs of the music industry and can provide support, direction, and critical comments when required.

4. **Adapt to Industry Changes:** The music industry is constantly evolving, and successful songwriters are adaptable and willing to change. Stay up-to-date on industry developments, technological breakthroughs, and changes in consumer behavior, and be prepared to adjust your approach to songwriting, promotion, and distribution accordingly. Accept new platforms, technology, and chances to reach audiences and engage with them in novel ways.

5. **Develop Resilience and Perseverance:** Long-term success in songwriting necessitates tenacity and endurance in the face of adversity, failure, and rejection. Recognize that failures are a normal part of the creative process and view them as chances for development and learning. Maintain a positive outlook, stay focused on your goals, and keep moving ahead even when faced with challenges or criticism.

6. **Improve business and marketing skills:** In addition to polishing your songwriting skills, learning business and

marketing techniques is critical for long-term success in the music industry. Learn about music publishing, copyright regulations, royalties, contracts, and other areas of the music industry so that you can safeguard your rights and optimize your earnings. Invest time in developing your brand, marketing your music, and connecting with your fans via social media, live concerts, and other platforms.

7. Be True to Your Artistic Vision: While it is necessary to be adaptive and receptive to input, it is also critical to maintain your artistic vision and creative integrity as a songwriter. Don't sacrifice your artistic vision or sincerity in the name of financial success. Focus on making music that speaks to you personally and connects with your listeners in a deeper way.

The Importance of Continual Learning and Growth

Starting a songwriting career is about more than just getting to a specific destination or level of success; it's also about a never-ending process of learning, growth, and personal development. Ongoing learning and development are crucial for aspiring songwriters just starting out.

Here's why:

1. Mastery of Craft: Continuous learning and development are required for mastering the craft of songwriting. Songwriting is a skill that requires consistent practice, experimentation, and refinement. By constantly learning new techniques, studying different song structures, and exploring different genres and styles, songwriters can improve their craft and create music that is both technically proficient and emotionally resonant.

2. Adaptability to Industry Changes: New technologies, platforms, and trends shape the way music is created, distributed, and consumed in the constantly evolving music industry. Songwriters who embrace a mindset of continual learning and growth are better equipped to adapt to these changes and stay relevant in an ever-changing industry. Whether it's learning how to navigate digital distribution platforms, mastering social media marketing

techniques, or understanding the complexities of music licensing and publishing, staying informed and adaptable is essential for success.

3. Inspiration and Creativity: Continuous learning and growth can serve as a source of inspiration and creativity for songwriters. Exposure to new ideas, experiences, and perspectives can spark creativity and fuel the songwriting process. Whether it's delving into different musical genres, exploring other art forms such as literature or visual arts, or learning about diverse cultures and traditions, the process of continual learning can broaden one's creative horizons and inspire new musical expressions.

4. Personal Development: Beyond the technical aspects of songwriting, continual learning and growth also contribute to personal development and self-discovery. Songwriting is a deeply personal and introspective endeavor that often requires songwriters to tap into their emotions, experiences, and innermost thoughts. Through the process of continual learning, songwriters have the opportunity to explore their own identities, beliefs, and values and to channel these insights into their music.

5. Building Resilience and Perseverance: Starting a songwriting career can be a challenging and sometimes daunting endeavor, with setbacks, rejection, and self-doubt being common experiences along the way. Continual learning and growth can help songwriters build

resilience and perseverance in the face of these challenges. By embracing a growth mindset and viewing setbacks as opportunities for learning and growth, songwriters can develop the resilience and determination needed to overcome obstacles and continue moving forward on their musical journey.

6. Connection with Audience: Continual learning and growth also play a crucial role in fostering a deeper connection with the audience. As songwriters evolve and grow, their music reflects their personal growth and experiences, making it more authentic and relatable to listeners. By continually honing their craft and exploring new musical territories, songwriters can create music that resonates with their audience on a deeper level, forging meaningful connections and leaving a lasting impact.

Overcoming Challenges in the Music Industry

Starting a songwriting career is a thrilling path full of unlimited potential, but it also has its own set of problems. Overcoming these obstacles is critical for aspiring songwriters to thrive in the competitive and always-changing music industry.

1. Self-Doubt and Criticism: One of the most typical difficulties that songwriters have is dealing with self-doubt and criticism. As they begin to share their music with the public, songwriters may receive unfavorable criticism or endure rejection, leading to questions about their skills and abilities. Overcoming self-doubt takes resilience, self-belief, and the determination to continue in the face of criticism. Songwriters may boost their confidence by concentrating on their abilities, getting constructive criticism, and reminding themselves of their love for music.

2. Finding Opportunity: Navigating the music industry and identifying possibilities for exposure and acclaim may be difficult for young songwriters. To get into the sector, you must be persistent, network, and plan strategically. Songwriters can overcome this problem by actively looking for venues to promote their work, such as open mic nights, songwriting competitions, music festivals, and internet platforms. Building contacts with industry professionals,

working with other musicians, and utilizing social media and digital marketing may all help songwriters broaden their reach and connect with their fans.

3. Financial constraints: Financial restraints are another major obstacle for many aspiring songwriters. Pursuing a music career sometimes necessitates significant expenses in equipment, recording sessions, marketing, and promotion. To circumvent financial restraints, songwriters should look into alternate funding alternatives such as crowd-funding campaigns, grants, sponsorships, or finding part-time work to supplement their musical activities. Budgeting and financial planning may also help songwriters manage their costs and prioritize investments in their music careers.

4. Balancing Creativity with Commercial Success: Many songwriters struggle to strike the right balance between creative integrity and economic success. While being loyal to one's creative vision is vital for creating original and meaningful music, songwriters must also consider market trends, audience preferences, and industry needs in order to achieve economic success. To overcome this problem, songwriters must find a balance between originality and financial viability, remaining faithful to their creative voice while also being willing to experiment with new genres, styles, and partnerships that appeal to a larger audience.

5. Competition and Oversaturation: The music industry is extremely competitive, with hundreds of young songwriters competing for attention and fame. Standing out in a competitive market takes originality, ingenuity, and tenacity. Songwriters may overcome this problem by concentrating on their own skills and voices, polishing their art, and creating a strong brand identity. Building a dedicated fan-base, communicating with listeners, and always refining their music may help songwriters stand out from the crowd and carve out a position in the market.

6. Rejects and Setbacks: Rejection and disappointment are unavoidable aspects of the music industry experience. Whether it's being rejected by record companies, music festivals, or receiving bad feedback, songwriters will undoubtedly suffer setbacks along the way. Overcoming rejection needs tenacity, perseverance, and an optimistic outlook. Songwriters can use setbacks to strengthen their craft and drive themselves to do better.

Nurturing Your Creativity and Passion

Nurturing your creativity and enthusiasm is critical to launching a successful songwriting career. Songwriting is a very personal and creative effort that involves delving into your deepest emotions, memories, and imagination.

Here are some ideas to cultivate your creativity and enthusiasm while embarking on your quest to become a songwriter:

1. Embrace inspiration. Creativity lives on inspiration; therefore, seek out varied sources of inspiration. Listen to a variety of music genres, read books, poetry, and literature, watch movies, experience nature, travel, and participate in activities that engage your senses and creativity. Be attentive to your surroundings and let daily events, emotions, and observations inspire you.

2. Establish a Creative Space: Create a specific creative environment where you can concentrate on composing without interruptions. Find a comfortable and inspiring environment, whether it's a quiet corner in your house, a private area in nature, or a neighborhood café. Surround yourself with items, pictures, and music that inspire you, and create an environment that encourages creativity.

3. Establish a Routine: Create a regular songwriting regimen to build discipline and consistency. Set aside time each day or week to concentrate on your music, whether it's writing lyrics, creating melodies, or trying out new ideas. Consistent practice is essential for polishing your trade and developing your creativity over time.

4. Embrace experimentation: Do not be scared to try out new songwriting techniques, styles, and approaches. Allow yourself to go into new musical territory, take creative chances, and push the limits of your comfort zone. Embrace the process of trial and error, and let setbacks or failures fuel your determination. Every experiment helps you improve as a songwriter and stimulates your creative journey.

5. Collaborate with Others: Collaboration with other musicians, songwriters, and artists may provide a great source of inspiration and innovation. Collaborative songwriting workshops allow you to share ideas, viewpoints, and experiences, resulting in fresh creative discoveries and expanded musical horizons. Collaborations also allow for mutual support, criticism, and encouragement, which fosters a sense of community and camaraderie throughout your creative journey.

6. Engage in self-care: Developing your creativity and enthusiasm demands taking care of your physical, mental, and emotional health. Make time for self-care activities like exercising, meditating,

writing, or spending time with family. Prioritize rest, relaxation, and activities that will replenish your creative energy and prevent burnout. Remember that creativity thrives in a healthy mind and body.

7. Maintain curiosity and open-mindedness: Maintain an inquisitive and open-minded approach to your creative process. Be open to new ideas, comments, and constructive criticism. Maintain your curiosity about new musical genres, styles, and approaches, as well as your willingness to learn and improve. Cultivate a lifelong learning and exploration mentality, seeking inspiration and challenging yourself to improve as a composer.

Balancing Artistic Integrity with Commercial Viability

Balancing creative integrity and financial feasibility is an important component of beginning a songwriting career. As a composer, you have a distinct artistic vision and voice that you wish to genuinely communicate via your songs.

However, you must also consider the business side of the music industry, including how to make your music accessible to a larger audience while remaining faithful to your artistic vision.

Understanding artistic integrity: Creative integrity is the dedication to expressing your true self via music without sacrificing your principles, beliefs, or creative vision. It entails staying true to your own voice, expressing your creativity, and creating music that reflects your personal experiences and emotions. Artistic integrity is critical for building a genuine connection with your audience and maintaining your credibility as an artist.

Navigating Commercial viability: Commercial viability, on the other hand, entails understanding market trends, audience preferences, and industry demands so that your music can reach a larger audience and generate revenue. This might include adding aspects from popular music genres, experimenting with alternative song structures, or working with other artists to create music that appeals to a wider audience.

Finding Balance: Finding the balance between creative integrity and financial feasibility is a tricky dance for songwriters. It requires careful consideration of your artistic objectives, audience preferences, and industry trends.

Here are some ideas for finding that balance:

1. **Understand Your Audience:** Understanding your target audience is vital for generating music that resonates with them while being loyal to your artistic vision. Research your audience demographics, musical interests, and listening patterns to personalize your music to their likes while preserving your distinctive style and voice.

2. **Collaborate Wisely:** Collaborating with other composers, producers, and performers may be a beneficial method to explore new creative ideas and reach a larger audience. Choose colleagues that share your artistic vision and beliefs while bringing fresh views and abilities to the table.

3. **Experiment with Genre and Style:** Don't be hesitant to explore diverse musical genres, styles, and inspirations in your songwriting. While staying true to your core artistic identity, exploring diverse musical territories can help you

discover new creative avenues and appeal to a broader audience.

4. **Embrace Feedback:** Receiving feedback from trusted peers, mentors, and industry professionals can offer valuable insights into the perception of your music and its commercial potential. Be open to constructive criticism while staying true to your artistic vision and values.

5. **Stay authentic:** Maintaining authenticity and sincerity in your music is crucial for building a genuine connection with your audience. Don't compromise your artistic integrity or values for the sake of commercial success. Stay true to yourself and your creative vision, and trust that your authenticity will resonate with your audience.

6. **Adapt to Industry Trends:** While staying true to your artistic vision, it's also important to adapt to industry trends and technological advancements. Stay informed about current music trends, streaming platforms, and digital marketing strategies to maximize your music's commercial potential while maintaining your artistic integrity.

7. **Be patient and persistent:** Finding the balance between artistic integrity and commercial viability takes time, patience, and persistence. Stay resilient in the face of setbacks or challenges along the way. Stay committed to

your craft, continue honing your skills, and trust in your unique voice as a songwriter.

Leaving a Lasting Impact: Legacy and Influence in Songwriting

As a songwriter, the desire to make a lasting impression through your music is a tremendous motivator that goes beyond monetary success. Leaving a legacy and inspiring people through your songs demonstrates the depth of your craft and the profound relationships you make with listeners.

Here's how you can create a legacy and impact through songwriting:

1. Authenticity and Vulnerability: Authenticity and vulnerability are essential components of crafting music that connects with people and has a long-lasting influence. By drawing on your own experiences, emotions, and truths, you may produce music that is authentic and accessible to listeners. Embrace your flaws and express them truthfully in your songwriting, since this transparency helps listeners connect with your music on a deeper level.

2. Universal Themes and Messages: Crafting songs with global themes and meanings guarantees that your music crosses cultural and generational borders, engaging with a wide range of people over

time. Love, sorrow, hope, and perseverance are ageless themes capable of eliciting strong emotions and stimulating thinking.

3. Honesty and Integrity: Maintaining honesty and integrity in your songwriting is critical for developing trust with your audience and leaving a lasting impression. Be loyal to yourself and your artistic vision, even if it involves addressing uncomfortable facts or questioning conventional standards. Your authenticity and integrity will be evident in your music, making a lasting impression on listeners who value your honesty and sincerity.

4. Social Commentary and Advocacy: Many renowned songwriters utilize their songs to raise awareness about social concerns, advocate for change, and initiate significant conversations. Whether it's confronting political injustice, campaigning for social equality, or raising awareness about mental health concerns, songwriters have the ability to influence good change through their songs. You may have a long-term influence on society and inspire people to take action by utilizing your music as a platform for social criticism and advocacy.

5. Innovation and Creativity: Pushing the boundaries of conventional songwriting and experimenting with new techniques and approaches might distinguish you as a visionary songwriter whose impact transcends standard genres and styles. Experiment with new sounds, unorthodox song structures, and collaborative

ventures that challenge the norm and encourage others to think beyond the box. Your desire to experiment and push new creative boundaries may leave a lasting legacy of musical brilliance and impact in the music business.

6. Mentorship and Collaboration: As your career advances, consider mentoring aspiring songwriters and working with new artists to share your expertise and encourage the next generation of musicians. Sharing your experiences, thoughts, and creative process with others allows you to leave a legacy of mentoring and cooperation, fostering a supportive and flourishing music community. Your role as a mentor and collaborator may help shape the careers of future songwriters and contribute to the continued growth of music as an art form.

7. Emotional Connection and Empathy: Finally, the greatest lasting legacies in songwriting are those that create profound emotional relationships with listeners, eliciting empathy and understanding. By tapping into the universal language of emotions and expressing empathy for the human situation, you may produce soulful music that makes a lasting impression on your audience's hearts and minds. Your ability to connect emotionally with listeners through your music reflects your history and influence as a songwriter.